P. M. S.

Poverty Mentality "lacking" Spirituality

P.M.S. SYNDROME: RE-DEFINED for the BLACK MIND

5

QUICK STRATEGIES

to Get Your MIND RIGHT so YOU can LIVE RIGHT!

MICHELLE WHITBY

P.M.S.
Poverty Mentality "lacking" Spirituality
P.M.S. SYNDROME: RE-DEFINED for the BLACK MIND
This book is written for inspirational purpose.

DISCLAIMER

This book is a non – medical, it claims no medicinal healing properties. It is intended for inspirational purposes only.

P.M.S.

Poverty Mentality "lacking" Spirituality

P.M. S. SYNDROME: RE-DEFINED for the BLACK MIND

5

QUICK STRATEGIES

to Get Your MIND RIGHT so You Can LIVE RIGHT!©

Is written in the belief that we as individuals have the capability to change our MIND-SETS. It is strictly intended for inspirational purposes of transforming lives. It is not intended to replace the need for medical treatment. I as the author make no claim to be a Psychologist or Dr in the field of Psychiatry who have the expertise to help heal mental illnesses. I recommend all who need mental health services seek specialized treatment with a medical professional accordingly.

I am Michelle, it is my intention to encourage and inspire all.

Contents

A Note of Infinite Thanks!

~

Thank you to friends and family numerous and dear to my heart (I wish I could name you all) for supporting me and joining me on this journey as I "Walk in my Destiny" to help others to know better, to do better so that they can transform their lives. This book is the first book of many that the DIVINE has blessed my mind with to write and share with others so that they too can "Walk In Their Destinies"

THANK YOU, THANK YOU, EVERYONE!

The following individuals a special recognition of thanks for your love, constant support, and encouragement.

Mom, Dad, Aunties, Sisters, Brothers, Nieces, Nephews, Cousins

Dr. Nicole Steele	*Beverly Carroll*
Dr. Cynthia Harper	*Shirley Reynolds*
Paisha A Brown	*Karen Lomax*
Betty Nappier	*Karen Parker*
Phyllis Mitchell	*Deborah Johnson*
Darlene Person	*Donna Satchell- Kimbell*
Lynda Shorter	*Msifiri Jorden Bey*
Gloria Parks	*Jonaye Ford*
	FeLicia Green-Carswell

Women Aspiring Together To Succeed / WATTS

*"GOD knows what he needs done on the earth
and how to get it done…
HE just may be calling YOU to do it…so listen up"!*

*I am Michelle
This is my Mantra*

Introduction

I am Michelle

This is my very first book to pen.

When the revelation came I simply started to write…

YOUR DIVINE CALL / KNOWLEDGE

A people in need of healing is what my spirit speaks to me. My dedication to answer the call.   I believe God talks to us ALL in some way, in some shape or form, my thing is what takes us soooooo long to answer the call? I really admire those that get it sooner more so than later, they know their life's purpose early on. I am definitely in the later crowd, at times I'm resentful, but truth of the matter is maybe I would not have been smart enough or wise enough to use the gifts that GOD has placed in me to use now. Maybe, just maybe my life is rolling out day by day, the way it is supposed to. Maybe this is the same for you? Before now maybe you had no reason to know or use the knowledge that you will obtain from this book. I believe that each and every day we are blessed to open our eyes and ears the Divine is whispering and constantly trying to get our attention and lead us in the right direction. Let me speak for myself, at least this has been the case for me. I often say

LORD what took me soooooo long! Gods perfect timing is all I can sum it up to be and maybe before now I was not ready to receive his DIVINE WORD. I have a DIVINE WORD for you, "if you are fortunate enough to be born in the USA then it is not Gods intention for YOU to REMAIN in POVERTY"!

The intention of this book is to inspire you to eliminate the poverty mentality of "Po mindset", "Po self - image", and "Po finances". My hope is that it will help take your thoughts from 'Po" to "Powerful" and that you will discover your super power within that will lead you to implement the changes you need to achieve the desires, gifts, or talents that the DIVINE has placed in you.

The Inspiration YOU need to Break Free and clear your mind from mental pain and transform your life !

DIVINE ORDER….
Your steps are ordered…
destiny you found this book, or it found you because you must……

1st …Save Yourself!

When this thought entered my mind, I knew that I would dedicate my life to writing…"Self -Therapy" Books because..

"YOU have to Save Yourself before
YOU can save anyone else."

Your Future is calling for KNOWLEDGE and possible CHANGE and you have answered the call by picking up this book of inspiration detailing 5 quick strategies to help you to break free of the poverty mentality that can keep you in mental pain and not living your best life. You have got to get your mind right so that you can live right!

I am amazed at what has been downloaded in my brain to share with you. I had no plan of writing such a book. This is a book of obedience I simply wrote what the DIVINE placed in my mind.

It is proof that God answers prayers.

A prayer answered immediately that revealed this P.M.S. meaning to me.

It was so clear in my mind and no doubt a revelation from the GREAT DIVINE!

If you are reading it, just know that the DIVINE has a revelation for you also.

Briefly I speak of the PMS meaning that most women know the long term for it is Premenstrual Syndrome. This is a syndrome of physical and mental pain, common symptoms are mood swings, depression, and poor concentration, irritabilities that rob most of us of our otherwise sensibilities.

The "Epiphany" given to me is PMS and P.M.S. symptoms are the same no matter your race, no matter your age, but if you are black there is an additional symptom called "lack". This is not a book about the deep psychological "chains" of slavery that even today remains. It instead is a book of inspiration offering 5 quick strategies to help you release the mental chains that keep you encaged. And this is why I have re-defined P.M.S. Syndrome of a special kind. It is ***P.M.S. SYNDROME of the BLACK MIND.***

This syndrome of which I specifically speak affects the
BLACK MENTALITY.

It is
P.M.S.
POVERTY MENTALITY "lacking" SPIRITUALITY™

It is a MINDSET that cannot see what the DIVINE
has called it to BE.

It is a MINDSET that negatively affects our CONFIDENCE.

It is a "POVERTY MENTALITY" keeping millions stuck in
unwanted realities.

Mental irritabilities that render you incapable of doing simple things. And if you cannot do the simple things you cannot conceive living outside your current realities. Because those negative thoughts in your head make living life such a dread. Dread cancels dreams that could become your (now) new reality.

It has been bugging me so, the struggles of black folks that just seems to grow and grow. I started to think about me personally somehow, I have been an escapee because I encounter the same P.M.S. pain (mood swings, occasional depression, at times poor concentration) yet somehow, I was able to break free from those mental chains that encaged me. And since the revelation that came, I have not been the same. The DIVINE revealed to me that it was my positive mentality.

Again, this ALL started with a prayer because I wanted to know how I have had such a good life in spite of it ALL.

This was the response whispered to me as I was awakened from a deep comatose sleep. The answer given to me in 3's and has led to this MIND/MENTALITY journey destination.

MINDSET
MINDSET
MINDSET

And this is what you will TEACH, your new assignment will be to encourage people out of the "POVERTY MENTALITY' and overcome the P.M.S. mental pain that keeps their MINDS in CHAINS.

When the revelation of what my MIND had done for me, I got busy writing and creating new DREAMS, one being that I would change 1 million MENTALITIES.

This is my P.M.S. story to encourage you to change YOUR MINDSET and be WHAT YOU ARE CALLED TO BE! GOD answers prayers and it is not his desire to have you poor and stuck in despair.

He has gifted you too! Quiet your MIND space so that he can reveal it to you!

This book will help you RE-SET your MINDSET

5 Quick Strategies ….

A remedy to
PMS and P.M.S.

Again, the same symptoms for both mood swings, depression, poor concentration, irritability, and if you are black an additional symptom called "lack".

It is the **Poverty Mentality "lacking" Spirituality** that keeps us stuck in an unwanted realities.

This book is for **ALL** because **I love ALL** but if you are black like me sometimes, we need a specialty. It is written specifically for us because the world tends to neglect us!

Today be thankful to the DIVINE because this is the day for you to RE-SET your mind and start living your prime!

I Affirm

YOU ARE AN AWESOME CHILD OF GOD.

MICHELLE WHITBY
Aspiring Author of "Self-Therapy" Books
I aspire to write books to first help me then to help you!

Sarah Young

*"YOU are being transformed from the inside out.
I form YOU into the one I desire YOU to be.
Hold my hand in childlike trust, and the way before
you will open up STEP BY STEP."*

January 25 Devotional
Jesus Calling
Enjoying Peace in His Presence

P. M. S.

Poverty Mentality "lacking" Spirituality
P.M.S. SYNDROME: RE-DEFINED for the BLACK MIND

5

QUICK STRATEGIES
to Get Your MIND RIGHT so YOU can LIVE RIGHT!

STRATEGY IN THE MAKING

If you bought this book or it was gifted to you, it is not by happen-stance, not by accident, but by DIVINE ORDER. Because you are a beloved child of the DIVINE CREATOR and you desire more this message was going to get to you no matter what!! I just happen to be the physical messenger of this spiritual message from our DIVINE CREATOR to "Get Your MIND RIGHT so YOU can LIVE RIGHT!" These 5 Strategies transform the syndrome of PMS and P.M.S. mood swings, depression, poor concentration, symptoms of mental pain that keep you encaged.

Before I get to the 5 Strategies, I must start with the revelation of the "5 STRATEGIES IN THE MAKING" by first sharing a true story that I hope encourages you.

The story begins with "Divine Order" words I heard many times and spoken by a friend, her official mantra! One day she spoke these words as usual but this particular day I heard them differently they were words that entered my ears as a whisper but penetrated my SOUL as if announced on a loudspeaker. These two words have become my focus, my creed. "Divine Order" a mantra I whole heartedly believe.

You are ready to reset your mindset your unconscious mind hears the whispers. Furthermore YOU are ready to get your life right and Divine Order directed you to me and if you tune in intentionally the DIVINE, the Divinity, the Universe, whatever term you use for your GOD "deity" will direct your next steps, all you have to do is to continue to listen and follow the lead.

Marinate on this:

You desire more than your current life situation, or you would not have made this purchase or received this gift. Yet something… you do not know who, why, or what DIVINTY lead you to me.

This little book will be the best five-dollar ($5) investment in yourself and when you improve YOU there are no limitations of what you can do. My instruction was to price this affordably so together we can sow seeds. What we do together is how we help one another. YOU "Getting Your MIND RIGHT so YOU Can LIVE RIGHT" is bigger than you and me there is a whole community at stake, souls dying as we speak. This is why DIVINITY/DIVINE ORDER instructed me to price it relatively cheap!

Once your friends and family recognize that you are determined to "Get YOUR Mind Right" you will inspire them to RE-SET their mindset. You see I am on a mission to change mindsets especially in the black community, I cannot do it alone for this **we must have unity**. What I witness today is some of the most brilliant of minds doing any and everything and mostly stuck in negativity. A "Poverty Mentality" this brilliant mind has forgotten that we come from a lineage of GREAT thinkers and creators of many GREAT things. I have encountered minds so rattled and shattered they just do not know what to believe, P.M.S. a **Poverty Mentality "lacking" Spirituality**, brilliant minds simply gone weak because it is listening to the wrong voices uttered in our society. Voices designed to keep brilliant minds in a state of confusion and living in a poverty state of delusion.

I decree YOU, me together… **we will change mindsets** from the "Poverty Mentality", as a community we cannot sit on the sidelines and do nothing as those who look like us, our once thought of brothers and sisters now kill each other. It is obvious that brilliant minds are believing the lies.

These minds must wake up and "Get Their MINDS RIGHT, so They Can LIVE RIGHT!" and stop believing the lies of society and get back to spirituality. It is the "Poverty Mentality" that hinders spirituality and without "Spirituality" YOU LIVE YOUR MENTALITY so if YOUR spirit is not in tune to the voice of GOD inside of YOU…YOU simply at times won't know what to do. You will remain with the P.M.S. pain that keep you encaged.

Shortly, I will officially introduce myself and why I believe "Divine Order" lead me to write this book and why I am confident that it will transform your mindset. It will cause you to intentionally plan and think your thoughts. Thoughts which are purposefully thought, along with actions taken will no doubt turn into manifestation.

This is WHY I BELIEVE DIVINE ORDER is always guiding me and YOU and has linked our destines, we have got work to do!

A Quick short…

BEFORE THE REVELATION OF THE 5 STRATEGIES…

My new MINDSET RE-SET journey begins, January 16, 2018 I Googled in every combination I could think of "Black Peoples Problems", "Black Peoples Issues", "The Struggle of Black People", "Why Do Black People Struggle So?". The results were basically NOTHING and I was simply dumb founded because in my mind Google answers everything! It listed a return of some stuff, yes, most about crimes committed, but not the answers I was looking for. So, me being the praying woman that I am, that night I said, "LORD WHY DO WE STRUGGLE SO, I NEED ANSWERS"?

My prayer was answered the very next morning as I was awakened from good sleep, I call it "comatose sleep". That good sleep was halted when suddenly I was awakened by unexplainable magical powers and its magic wand sat me straight up and spoke to my mind as if on a loudspeaker MINDSET, MINDSET, MINDSET. Yes, it was repeated 3 times just like that.

This voice reminded me of how I have been able to live such a good life. The answer, this revelation changed the trajectory of everything for me. The DIVINE magical powers spoke to me and I realized that before we can get to our dreams, we have to fix our "Mentalities". This led me to work on my own "Mentality" intentionally.

The Poverty Mentality "lacks" Spirituality, and this is what keeps us stuck! It is a syndrome of symptoms that affects our mental. Again, mood swings, depression, and poor concentration, P.M.S. pain that keep us encaged. This mind has forgotten its "Positive Purpose" functionality. Repeatedly, listening to the wrong negative voices and influences of this society. It has chosen to deny "Spirituality" and instruction from the CREATOR and do its own thing.

When the "Epiphany" hit me of what my mindset had done for me on a small scale...which was to keep me out of the housing projects. I believe God birthed in me a new MINDSET, a new MENTALITY, a new INSIGHT into this poverty mentality and that is before we can pursue BIG DREAMS… We first must "Get Our Minds Right" once we "Get Our Minds Right" (by eliminating drama, depression, mood swings, and other negativities) we can "Live Right". Additional insight, when we "Live Right, we Focus Right" and the "Right Focus" is what will lead all to be who they are meant to be. The "Right Focus" is on Gods instruction and not this societies.

I am thankful again for this "Epiphany" because I never really believed to be stuck in poverty would be my future. Once more, I've had a good life for having come out of the projects, but I now realize that I can have an even better life based on my AWAKENED MINDSET, so I immediately got busy thinking BIG thoughts and BIG new DREAMS!

This is why I have the audacity to believe that I can change 1 million mindsets from "Poverty" to "Purpose Mentality". In other words from "Po" to "Powerful" and for this reason I proudly boast I am the "Po" Peoples Coach!

Yes, a new mission given specifically to me to lead to help others tear down, counter act and get rid of the P. M.S. **Poverty Mentality "lacking" Spirituality** and eliminate the mental pain that keep us encaged.

The "Poverty Mentality" does not solely exist in those who are financially challenged it exist in all kinds of minds. It is a mindset stuck in fear, it is a mindset simply stuck, it is a mindset muddled in muck. It is a mindset that believes that it is entitled to only meager things. It is the mind of the negative kind.

I am Michelle, I escaped poverty and a whole host of other issues simply because of my "beliefs" …and a "Mentality" that embraces my "Spirituality". I believe that in spite of all my life challenges I can, and I will overcome the "Poverty Mentality" I too have to "Get and KEEP My Mind

Right so that I can Live Right!" I will *conquer* this poverty mentality! It will not rob me of who I am meant to be.

The DIVINE God has made promises that he guarantees he will keep!

Two Bible verses that come to mind and that has always helped me.

"We are more than conquerors"
Romans 8:37

and

"The thief comes only to steal and kill and destroy.
I came that they may have life
and have it abundantly."
John 10:10

These 2 promises I whole heartedly believe.

From an incredibly young age I have always believed in God a higher being than me, in other words DIVINE DIVINITY that leads me spiritually.

Despite what I was born into which was much family dysfunction I have always believed beyond the "Poverty Mentality". There was always a voice or a whisper that spoke to me often telling me I was smart enough not to stay poor and in the housing projects. I just never held onto the "Poverty Mentality" which was my childhood reality. As a small child I envisioned a Bigger Life and I would talk to God, a conversation that always felt right. I was reciting affirmations out loud and did not know that I was training my brain in what to believe. I had no idea I was creating a positive "Mentality", my own actuality.

Confidently, and often out loud I would say to my friends "y'all know I love YOU, right…but I'm not staying here with y'all forever in the projects"! "I've got places to go and people to see" …..now I had no clue where I was going and who I was going to see. I just knew a life of poverty was not my destiny.

So, you see I have been on this journey all along, but I've often lost focus. Thankfully, the DIVINE has sharpened my mind. My prayer has been answered the MINDSET, MINDSET, MINDSET this revelation leads me to take brand new actions. It confirmed for me that we are literally what we THINK! I know what my MINDSET has done for me and I have started to think of everything differently **intentionally.**

Strategies and thoughts of how I could teach others and encourage them to change their mindsets so we can RE-DREAM together! Can you imagine being life-long supporters of each other's dreams? This would mean an **infinite number of possibilities.**

Imagine YOU like me being born for such a time as this. YOU at some point in time have thought about a better life…a DIVINE thought placed intentionally in your mind, but a thought you could not hold onto for a long period of time. As time passes, we cannot conceive our dominate thoughts lead our destiny. **Whether negative or positive what we focus on becomes our creed**!

Just think YOU or someone did it for YOU, purchased a five-dollar ($5) book to get you started on a new journey to RE-THINK your thoughts so you can "Get Your MIND RIGHT" to live a better life and truly live YOUR God given dreams. I believe its our God given dreams that propels us to succeed.

I am so excited for you I could run around and scream. God has placed in me the passion and desire to help people but especially my people to be better human beings and to move past fear and eliminate the P.M.S. mental pain that keep them encaged. You have got to Get your MIND RIGHT to live YOUR best life!

When I was given this vision, the "Epiphany" to write a book about actual strategies to help change mindsets that will transform lives, the first thought that came to mind was to make it affordable. Thus, as DIVINE ORDER would have it the very first price that came to mind was five dollars ($5).

YES, just five dollars ($5) which I know this tiny seed in one's self is the start to many dynamic things presently unseen so obediently I listened to DIVINE instruction this little book will be the first of many others.

But with the price came thoughts of struggle because I continued to think about that five-dollar ($5) amount and the human being that I am I **EDGED GOD OUT**. In my EGO, the selfish dominate mind, just that quick I inflated the price. Seven dollars ($7) and then ten dollars ($10) came to mind, no way my EGO said "could this book be the five-dollar ($5) price. In the end I am thankful for the DIVINE in my mind. I believe his way is better than mine, so I proceeded with this five-dollar ($5) price.

A SNIPPET of STRATEGY #1

MY ENCOURAGEMENT FOR YOU TO LISTEN TO THE DIVINE VOICE THAT GUIDES YOU!

LISTEN, SEE, TRUST and BELIEVE – Listen to your positive thoughts do not take them likely. You have to listen to the lead, your spirituality, (the 1st thought is usually the right thought implanted in your mind by the DIVINE). It is the first thought that your MIND eye sees. This is usually almost always the case with me! The day of the $5 book "thought", I received an immediate confirmation in regard to confirming the price…this is a quick and true story that I hope encourages you to LISTEN, SEE, TRUST and BELIEVE.

Check this out I am running late for work, finally out of the house and in the car, the first thing I do is turn on the radio (which is not my normal routine), but as Divine Order would have it … the announcement being made over and over was the $5 cost of things! The advertisement was $5 admission to get into the club and $5 drinks. I knew without a doubt this was a sign for me. The $5 YOU paid for this book or someone paid for YOU is going to lead you on a journey you would not believe. This is my MINDSET I LISTEN, SEE…I TRUST, and I BELIEVE. This book I was instructed is just the first of many seeds that will be sown into others encouraging them to RE-SET their MINDS so they can transform their lives and get over P.M.S. pain that keep them encaged.

More of my LISTEN, SEE, TRUST and BELIEVE journey:

- Born in Cincinnati, Ohio to a single mother of five who only had a 9th grade education.

- I knew of my biological father but had no personal relationship with him.

- I had a great stepdad when he was not drinking and drunk. He has been sober now too many years to count. I would not trade him for the world.

- I was sexually molested as a small child.

- Grew up and married the first person who told me he loved me. He was the wrong person. Divorce was inevitable it was a domestic violence situation.

- I Married the 2nd wrong man. Divorce # 2 almost broke me. In my mind I just knew this marriage of 18 years was for life! I was about to quit working on my dreams. During this time I was LISTENING, SEEING and BELIEVING the wrong things. I was listening to the negative mental thoughts leading me to think less about who God created me to be. I was about to get stuck in muck that could have messed my life up! I started to believe I was a lessor human being because he no longer loved me. My focus was on the negativity that was sure to become my creed. The record playing constant in my mind was "look what he's done to poor little old me". Truthfully, the ugly things that happened during this time could have permanently messed up my mind. I was discouraged but I always managed to hold onto a glimmer of hope. It was a little dim light inside that led me back to the positive MIND.

-   Somewhere within me, I had to dig deep, I said to myself "I've got to re-focus and get back to my spiritualty" and I remembered that GOD has always been my lead! Bottom line, I have to face my own accountability and simply get over this major SELF PITY PARTY STORY.

Thankfully, my mind recalled the DIVINES words…
Deuteronomy 31:6 "He will never leave us or forsake us."

I snapped out of the Divorce #2 drama and the…
"I'm forever broken mentality". I had to deal with and eliminate the P.M.S. pain that could keep me encaged!

Talking about steps being ordered, DIVINE ORDER!

THE NEW JOURNEY BEGINS

Let me share with you how life works for a child of GOD with the right mindset and beliefs. Crisis for us do not last forever, although our negative thoughts or mindset will tell us otherwise.

- One of my 1st thoughts and eventually prayers – Lord I need a job so that I can take care of me and my daughter and not live in the projects!

- Lord I need I stress free job that will allow me to continue to work on me and to do those things you have put into me to do!

Well my prayers were answered, eventually (months passed) and at the same time quickly the whole trajectory of my life changed!

I must share in detail because we are now linked in destiny.

My stress-free job was in another state – hallelujah GOD removed me from the drama of a divorce scene. I did not see this job COMING! All the job rejections prior to this…this was the job waiting just for me.

This is the timeline of events that has led YOU to me so that I can encourage YOU to get your MIND right which in turn gets your LIFE right so that YOU can pursue your dreams.

- September 2017 – A new job in a new city. God knew exactly what I needed, DIVINE ORDER.

- December 2017 – End of the month around Christmas time I find myself in the bookstore. I have always been drawn to books. The book whispering to me no calling my name loudly THINK AND GROW RICH by NAPOLEON HILL. I pondered, I walked away, but the force would not let me leave that book on the shelf. I even said to myself I know I have this book I know that I have read it already. Then finally, I concluded because the force drawing me in would not quit, I looked at the price, just $7, what the heck "get the book and go"!

- January 2, 2018 – Early am, "I am an awesome child of God" my first thought of the year and I decided this would be my focus for 2018. I encourage you NOW to say it out loud. These words of affirmation I find to be an instant confidence booster.

- January 4, 2018 – The 3 M's (Mission, Mindset, and Mental Cleanse) the topic the guest speaker on the Black CEO Morning Show was addressing the moment I tuned in. **If you are like me, you wonder what in the heck is a Mental Cleanse? DIVINE ORDER…my steps being ordered briefly it is the practice of silencing the noise, clearing out clutter and negativity during this time focus only on the positive during this 30-day period RE-BOOT the brain and RE-THINK!** This practice turned out to be the life changing. I surpassed my initial commitment of 21 days. I was at 30+ days before I knew it and during this time unlike any other silent time in my life, I could clearly hear the voice whispering to me. Never so CLEARLY could I LISTEN, RE-THINK and RE-DREAM. I experienced an explosion of positive thoughts. My MINDSET was elevated, numerous business ideas and ideas of how I could help others came to my mind. It was to the point where I could hardly put down pen and paper. It was fun (running around the house talking to myself and trying to write down everything), exciting, yet scary because my mindset was elevated to a higher degree and I knew this would require more of me.

- January 6-7, 2018 – The Diamond In The Rough Royal Women's Retreat that I have attended at the first of every year for the last couple of years. Well DIVINE ORDER…my steps being ordered; this year's theme was the awesome reminder that I needed at this point and stage in my life to remind me to **"walk in my destiny"**. A feat I was clearly ready to take on especially after learning of a Mental Cleanse.

- January 15, 2018 - BACK to the BLACK CEO Radio Show…this time it is an evening CALL, 7PM to be exact, I hesitate but I jump on. The discussion I catch…"2018 will be EPIC – WE WILL USE OUR COLLABORATIVE MUSCLE TO STRENGTHEN OUR COMMUNITY"! "Today's call – How do we help build up EVERYONE who is a part of the Black CEO movement"? And then she speaks the messenger for me that day! She starts out by saying she has AUDACIOUS FAITH! Immediately I perk up and I'm encouraged to have what she has which is AUDACIOUS FAITH! **Per Dictionary.com …AUDACIOUS – Extremely BOLD or DARING: Fearless extremely organic.** Yes, with my renewed mindset that is me!

- January 16, 2018 – I am all pumped the THINK and GROW RICH principles have started to penetrate my mindset, I am all in, I have a renewed faith AUDACIOUS FAITH…. yet there is still 1 thing egging at me that keeps me unsettled…I shared it at the beginning of the book, and I repeat it here because I really want you to get it…. *I question WHY do we struggle so as a people? How is it that I have had such a good life compared to others?*

In search of answers I went to GOOGLER
(as Wendy Williams calls it) and this is what I keyed
"BLACK PEOPLES PROBLEMS"
in every combination I could think of!

My return of an answer was basically NOTHING! I stared at the screen, tried to dig deeper by going to web pages 5 and 6, I was truly dumb founded because the GOOGLER usually has the answers to everything!

- January 17, 2018 - Thankfully, I did not have to wait long for an answer because this is the day I was awaken out of a deep comatose sleep. It was as if magical powers were directing me. In my mind I was literally being raised from the dead and the words spoken into my head… MINDSET, MINDSET, MINDSET.

It was my MINDSET and belief in GOD that had saved me!

This was the answer to my prayer and the great revelation to me during this quiet time in my life this is to be what **I will go forward and teach others how to RE-SET their MINDSET.** This is how I am going to help my people see past the struggle of everyday life so they can release the mental pain that keeps them encaged. I will teach them what I know so that they can know better to do better. The first step of this process is they must "Get Their Minds Right" and together we can recreate new lives, ultimately new dreams.

This is how I'm going to motivate 1 million minds out of P.M.S. which is the **"Poverty Mentality "lacking" Spirituality".** It is symptoms of mental pain that keeps us encaged because we have settled for meager lives that are not led by the DIVINE.

I am Michelle

This is my P. M. S. Strategy…

to help you start today the process of re-setting your mind. You've got "to Get YOUR MIND RIGHT so that YOU can LIVE RIGHT!"

SHIFT YOUR MIND so that YOU can LIVE YOUR PRIME!

I have been in this positive mindset state of mind most of my life and did not know it or its power. January 2018, I paused and hit RE-SET!

You can do it too no matter your age! Do not delay another day, the sooner you start the sooner you will be on your way. Don't worry about the many steps just take the 2nd step you have already taken the 1st by purchasing or being gifted a little book on P.M.S. that you did not see coming. Every day that you are blessed to open your eyes it is the DIVINE giving you yet another opportunity to get it right! All the things that you have gone through will only help you!

It is DIVINE ORDER, remember your steps are already ordered.

"The steps of a man are established by the LORD, when he delights in his way…"
Psalms 37: 23-24

"The heart of a man plans his way, but the LORD establishes his steps."
Proverbs 16:9

"A man's steps are from the LORD; how can man understand his way?"
Proverbs 20:24

Stepping forward with the RIGHT MINDSET is all that is required of you, there are many more great life events waiting for YOU to step into. All you are required to do is to MOVE and TAKE ACTION on those things the DIVINE has placed in YOUR MIND. He wants you to RE-SET your MIND so that you can live RIGHT!

"Commit your way to the LORD;

trust in him, and he will act."

Psalm 37:5

THE 5 STRATEGIES IN ACTION

IN ESSENCE THE 5 STEPS NECESSARY TO HELP YOU ALONG YOUR TRANSFORMATIONAL JOURNEY.

Strategy – as defined by Dictionary.com

A plan, a method, or series of maneuvers or stratagems for obtaining a specific goal or result.

P. M.S. Strategy #1

of Get Your MIND RIGHT so YOU can LIVE RIGHT!

SILENCE THE NOISE
(Commit to 21 days of Silence)

John 10:27
My sheep hear my voice, and I know them, and they follow me.

The first and MOST IMPORTANT Strategy is to silence your atmosphere.

SILENCE……
SHUT OUT, SHUT DOWN, SHUT OFF, UNPLUG, CAGE, CLOSE DOWN, WALL OFF, SEAL OUT, BLOCK OUT, OBSTRUCT, TERMINATE, DETACH, GET RID of ALL unnecessary noise. This must be done if you are going to RE-SET so that you can LISTEN, SEE, TRUST, and form new BELIEFS.

SILENCING YOUR ATOMOSPHERE….

This involves discipline and obedience, IT WILL NOT BE EASY, but it is VITAL as this is your first step to prepping and elevating your mind. What needs to enter your mind cannot get to you and RE-ORDER YOUR STEPS if you do not silence the noise and sit in it!

If you want to be successful in implementing the other 4 Strategies, then you must start here. Get ready to experience CLARITY and an EXPLOSION of THOUGHTS unlike you have ever experienced before.

I too had to silence the noise and sit in it!
The experts say it takes 21 days to form a new habit – This was my initial commitment. I was afraid to commit to 30 days, no way, my EGO (**E**dging **G**od **O**ut) screamed. I am a living witness today I surpassed 21 days without thinking about it.   Because what was being fed to my MIND during this time was more important than what my MIND was being fed through the TV and other means.

When you silence the noise **TRUST** every positive thought be prepared to write them down. **HEAR** the new thought/s (it may be a whisper), **SEE** the new thoughts (new visuals may come to mind), and **BELIEVE** the new thoughts (DIVINE ORDER or RE-ORDER).

You have taken the 1st STEP to RE-SET YOUR MINDSET

The 1ST STRATEGY AGAIN, SILENCE THE NOISE SO YOU CAN HEAR RIGHT, SEE RIGHT, THINK RIGHT!

If you have never recited or been in the habit of reciting AFFIRMATIONS, start now!

Bonus Tip: I will share what immediately boost me and speaks to my confidence and I promise it will speak positively to YOU! Insert your name below

"I ________________________________ *am an AWESOME CHILD OF GOD*"

More specifically:

"I ________________________________ *am an AWESOME CHILD OF GOD" I have taken the 1st step and have silenced the noise. My steps are being ordered by the LORD. I can now clearly hear his voice; I know that I was "fearfully and wonderfully made" (Psalms 139:14) and I am clear or getting clearer that I was created to…*

____

____

____

____

____

"Whoever heeds instruction is on the path to life…"

Proverbs 10:17

P. M.S. Strategy #2

of Get Your MIND RIGHT so YOU can LIVE RIGHT!

PREPARE TO WRITE, WRITE, WRITE

Proverbs 29:18
Where there is no vision, the people perish: but he
that keepeth the law happy is HE.

You have taken the 1st action, by implementing Strategy #1 YOU HAVE SILENCED THE NOISE. **Now be prepared to record and WRITE because you will have an explosion of new thoughts and ideas enter your head.** Those gifts DIVINELY planted within your mind will rise to your consciousness.

Listen to me **NOW! PREPARE EVERY SPACE** with pencils, pens, note pads, sticky notes which ever you prefer. Place these items all over your house, in your car, in your pockets, ladies in your purse, **everywhere!** I want you to be prepared to write **IT** down. The thought or many new thoughts are coming to your mind for a reason. The plethora of thoughts exploding in your mind may not make sense now, but I assure you they will at some given time **so heed my instruction and prepare to write them down.**

DIVINE ORDER remember, you have been in struggle mode, and the voice you need to hear to help you could not get to you because you had too many other voices directing you. So again, PREPARE ALL YOUR SPACES for **the one and only voice, the most important voice you need to hear from which is from the inner you, the "GOD in you will come through**. It has been there all along wanting to speak to YOU!

I do not want you to miss a thing, no matter how small you think it is. **If a positive thought comes write it down or it will slip out of sight and then out of mind.** These written words spoken directly to you will remind you of what you need to resurrect or something of importance to do. This process will help you to record your vision so that it becomes clear. This is the 2nd strategy to help you get your mind right and focus on who you are becoming because the new thoughts in your mind is the voice of the DIVINE.

Remember what you **FOCUS** on is what will manifest, this is GODS universal law, not my law. GODS law as written, in the Bible (the ultimate instructional guide) tells us specifically what we should focus on and exactly what to do. It tells us everything we need to know! Again, my revelation as to why we struggle so is MINDSET,

MINDSET, MINDSET and what I have recently learned from the Bible 1st Corinthians 2:16, *But we have the MIND of CHRIST.* An epiphany that spoke LOUD to me…**But we have the MIND OF CHRIST!** So why do our MINDS forget?

Somewhere along the way as we live our lives, we get outside of the DIVINES MINDSET and memory loss of GODS LAW causes us to develop the WRONG FOCUS. Then we wonder why what we want in our lives does not manifest or simply that our lives are a mess! His word says, "he will never leave us or forsake us" *(Hebrews 13:5)*, but he will negate us because we negate him (deny or forget his existence). And those things we desire could possibly be denied or not come to our minds without the direction of the DIVINE.

GODS LAW requires us to tend to our MINDSETS EVERYDAY!

Quite frankly if we do not due to life's busyness we may forget what the Divine has placed in our minds.

Daily we are to work on our minds if we want to "Get our MINDS RIGHT so WE can LIVE RIGHT!"

The first 2 Quick Strategies help accomplish this law:

P.M.S. Strategy #1
SILIENCE THE NOISE

P.M.S. Strategy #2
WRITE or RECORD
what the
Divine voice speaks to your mind.

EVERYDAY!

*"...but **be ye transformed** by the renewing of YOUR MIND."*

Romans 12:2 (KJV)

*"And be not conformed to this world: but be ye transformed by the **renewing of your mind,** that ye may prove what is that good, and acceptable, and perfect, will of God."*

Romans 12:2 (KJV) King James Version

*"Do not be conformed to this world, but be transformed by the **renewal of your mind,** that by testing you may discern what is the will of GOD, what is good, and acceptable, and perfect."*

Romans 12:2 (TGI) The Gideons International

*"Do not act like the sinful people of the world. **Let God change your life.** First of all, **let Him give you a new mind.** Then you will know what God wants you to do. And the things you do will be good and pleasing and perfect."*

Romans 12:2 (NLV) New Life Version

"BUT We have the Mind of Christ"
1st Corinthians 2:16

P. M.S. Strategy #3
of Get Your MIND RIGHT so YOU can LIVE RIGHT!

READ, READ, READ

A primary way GOD speaks to us is through his
WORD or others words.

John 1:1
In the beginning was the WORD
and the WORD was with GOD, and the WORD was GOD.

My suggestion is read everything that is positive and that will TEACH! No matter what types of reading you are drawn to READ, READ, READ and not just books but everything! There is so much literature for us to learn from… newspapers, business magazines, sports magazines, blogs, essays, recipes, poetry, biographies, brochures, listen to audio books and especially read the BIG "B' book. The Bible which is the ultimate READ and instructional guide for our lives. It is evident as myself and so many others quote from it over and over.

Strategy #3 - I can sum it up quick, JUNK IN = JUNK OUT! And during this quiet time of your life you are RE-SETTING your mindset and allowing Gods words to saturate it.

You are ridding yourself of ALL the JUNK that YOU have allowed INTO YOUR MIND. Again, you are eliminating the P.M.S. mental pain that keep you encaged. **It is YOUR duty, no OBLIGATION TO PUSH MENTAL PAIN OUT!** This can only be done with POSITIVE REINFORCEMENTS! The WORD, many WORDS were written for a reason, not just to be pretty on a page and looked at, but to help YOU stay in the RIGHT MINDSET, YOUR #1 ASSET!

The good LORD, the first to have FOLLOWERS knew what he was doing when he instructed many of **his followers** to WRITE the way so that we could read from a permanent record and learn on our own. He is omnipotent (all knowing) and already knew in this age of "TECH FOLLOW" many of us, would get lost in the sauce. So, way before the use of today's technological driven world and the use of the term "Follow Me" on my Insta, Twit, or whichever social media platform he knew we would need the original text to turn back to.

Again, the DIVINE in all his omnipresence knows we are all at different levels of MINDS and has allowed mankind to develop ALL kinds of READING INSTRUCTION to help us no matter what our level of intelligence.

My book and so many others are here to guide you and to give you instruction, trust and believe the Bible is my 1st and many others lead. If it is a little too profound for your mindset right now, no worries GODS messengers know how to break it down and give it to you the way GOD instructs them to do! You may not reference the Bible right now, but make sure you own one because it is the "authentic" know how book of instruction. It confirms everything you do and remember the new mindset is directing you.

Meanwhile, no matter what level your mentality I have listed on the following page some READ ready recommendations to help you stay focused and keep you on track. You are to daily eliminate distractions that will try to turn your mindset back or keep you stuck in struggle because your mental strength is at a low level.

I must start with me, and of course you are already reading me – My instruction from the DIVINE is for me to write "quickies" in other words quick books to inspire your mind.

His other messengers of instruction, whom I like to refer to as "great minds of the DIVINE" are also blessed to help you deal with the mess of P.M.S. the mood swings, depression, and poor concentration. The symptoms of mental pain that keeps you encaged and dominate your mind from hearing the DIVINE. In other words, Poverty Mentality "lacking" Spirituality.

READ, READ, READ any and / or ALL of these!

Author	Book Title
Sarah Young	Jesus is Calling, Enjoying Peace in His Presence
Dr K. Shelette Stewart	Revelations in Business
Dr. Nicole Steele	PRICELESS: A Girls Guide to Uncovering, The Beauty, Boldness and Brilliance Within
Donna Satchell Kimble	Just Get Serious About Success
Cynthia Harper	Life on Purpose (Three Seasons) Reason, Season and Lifetime
Paulo Coelho	The Alchemist
DeYonne Parker	Girl Get Your S.W.A.G. Back! A Soul Freeing Journey for Women
Napoleon Hill	Think and Grow Rich
Millicent St. Claire	Simply Ridiculous, A Realization and Transformation of Ridiculous Beliefs and Behaviors
Brian Tracy	NO EXCUSES! The Power of Self Discipline
Don Miguel Ruiz	The Four Agreements
Scott Shickler & Jeff Waller	The 7 Mindsets to Live Your Ultimate Life
John Maxwell	Intentional Living Choosing a Life That Matters
Joyce Meyer	The Confident Woman Devotional
Pamela Adams	God is in Your Inbox, Inspirational Stories Shared through Your Everyday E-Mail
Minoka Smith	A Family Circle of Generation Curses
Pastor Gregory Dickow	Fast From Wrong Thinking
Dr. Na'im Akbar	Breaking the Chains of Psychological Slavery
George C. Fraser	Success Runs in Our Race

GODS WORD IS EVERYWHERE, and IT WILL SPEAK TO YOU!

Dr Charles Stanley

"Without His guidance, our MINDS become vulnerable to lies. The WORD of God is a compass that keeps us headed in the right direction, even in the midst of confusing messages.
The WORD is our guidebook."

INTOUCH
DAILY READING FOR DEVOTIONAL LIVING
JANUARY 30, 2019

P. M.S. Strategy #4
of Get Your MIND RIGHT so YOU can LIVE RIGHT!

START YOUR LIST of MVC'S
(Your Most Valuable Connections)

These are the people YOU are going to help
and the PEOPLE who are going to help you.

You sow seeds and people will sow into YOU! The
DIVINE'S Universal Law!

Family, Friends, Invisible Counselors, People you would like to
mingle with 1 day. Write their names down and say them out loud!

Your new MINDSET is guiding you to a new crew
that will keep you encouraged in the new things you do. God
is wanting to do a new thing so **out with the OLD** and **in
with the NEW.** This does not mean that you do not love your
family or value your relationships of longevity with friends
from your youth. You need these people and new
connections that encourage you to be the BEST YOU! So,
start a list and write down your MVC's and include anyone
new that you would want to meet. Writing them down helps
you to stay focused on your new mindset and helps ignite
new dreams. If you are like me, thinking, plotting, and
planning intentionally a new circle of friends your new
MINDSET focuses on all the possibilities.

If you have implemented Strategies 1-3 there is no doubt that your renewed mind is now directing you, don't be afraid, listen to the whispers of positivity from the DIVINE.

It's just YOUR new MINDSET and it is what is guiding you to new things with new people who are destined to help you. You are releasing the mental P.M.S. pain that once had you encaged. You realize you are not alone and its only with the help of others that we sincerely grow and keep our MINDSETS in check.

FURTHER INSTRUCTION…

Additionally, look for some new positive groups to get yourself into. Remember you need a new crew to encourage you and to help you develop in the new things God has for you to do.

I highly recommend these or start a group of your own:

Organization Name / What they Do / How they Help YOU!

E.L.L.E. Ebony Ladies Literary Experience
A Book Club I founded because I love to read, and I wanted to discuss books with ladies who represent me in color. If no existing book club is calling your name, I recommend you start your own!

TOAST MASTERS
https://www.toastmasters.org
The Public Speakers Masters, the name says it all.
This is an organization dedicated to help you
improve your public speaking skills. If you are like
me, you may be a little shy in this area but believe
somewhere within there is a speaker who is ready to speak to
the world what the DIVINE has placed in your mind and his
revelation to you of the great things he has for YOU to do!

MOCHA MOMS
https://www.mochamoms.org
This is an organization that is committed to MOMS of Color
to help them along their mommy hood journey by providing
support in so many ways. Their focus is on keeping moms
encouraged and focused on their self-development. It is a
national organization and a great place to meet new positive
friends. When I was a new mom, I do not know what I would
have done without MOCHA MOMS.

WATTS (Women Aspiring Together to Succeed)
https://wattsatlanta.weebly.com
An Atlanta Georgia organization that has been in existence
now for 15+ years for which I am honored to be a part of. It
was definitely Divine Order that lead me to this organization
of dynamic women because the person who invited me to the
first WATTS gathering that I attended never showed up! I
have been encouraged and connecting with this positive
group of ladies ever since my first meeting back in 2007.

DIAMOND IN THE ROUGH
https://ditr.org

DITR, is an award winning, youth development and leadership program dedicated to "Transforming the world . . . One Child, One Family, One Community at a time". DITR offers a variety of preventative programs and enrichment activities designed to build self-esteem, character, and leadership among girls of all ages. I have been a proud supporter and volunteer for the organization for 10+ years.

These are the organizations that have encouraged me and has helped me to be all that I can be. Now it is up to you to find and join positive support organizations that help you be the best YOU! "Seek and ye shall find" those opportunities orchestrated by the Divine to keep you encouraged and help to alleviate the P.M.S. mental pain that keep you encaged and not living what the Divine has place in your mind.

"Where there is no guidance, a people falls, but in an abundance of counselors there is safety."

Proverbs 11:14

P. M.S. Strategy #5

of Get Your MIND RIGHT So YOU can LIVE RIGHT!

Learn F. N. I. T.

Learn Fun, New, Interesting Things!

John 10:10
I came that they may have life and have it abundantly.

Learning and human development simply never stops, and it behooves you to continually do the work needed to improve you. Commit to **F.N.I.T.** and pursue to **Learn** and find **New, Fun, Interesting Things** that continue to develop your mind.

I would love to continue to walk with you through your transformational MINDSET RE-SET journey. I would be honored to host a "Mentality Workshop" for you and your crew. I shall call it specifically "Break FREE of the P.M.S. Mental Pain that Keep YOU Encaged™". It is designed to help you bury some struggles you have gone through and keep you focused on those things the DIVINE has placed in your mind.

Additionally, I am a proponent of keeping positive visuals before my eyes to keep me focused on what the DIVINE has placed in my mind. I have recently created a

"Focus Board" similar to a "Vision Board" it keeps the new re-imagined life vision before you. Those things we focus on tends to become our creed! If we focus on the symptoms of P.M.S. mental pain which are mood swings, depression, and poor concentration trust and believe this will be the outcome. There are so many things swirling around in our heads and loosing focus is easy to do. We must on a daily basis be vigilant about the MIND FULL of things positive or negative in our head and if we are not careful or MINDFUL our HEADS literally lead us toward the dominant thoughts in our minds.

In conclusion a "Poverty Mentality lacking Spirituality" will keep you in confusion or a state of mental delusion, implement the strategies and BREAK FREE OF THE P.M.S. PAIN THAT KEEP YOU ENCAGED!

I know the DIVINE will continue to bless you on your transformational journey. I am so GRATEFUL that I get to support you. And I thank you for helping me as I too pursue those things that the DIVINE has placed in me.

I have shared **the 5 Quick Strategies that I have lived**, and I am certain if implemented they will help you to…

Get Your MIND RIGHT so YOU can LIVE RIGHT!

I am Michelle, An Awesome Child of God and so are YOU!

Epilogue

TRUE CONFESSIONS

An additional note of encouragement for YOU

I almost quit on writing this book about P.M.S. my FOCUS was on the wrong things and was going to allow fear and doubt to forfeit my destiny. I had started to write this book at the beginning of 2018 and somewhere along the way my mind started to sway, I was letting the drama of divorce get in the way. I stopped writing and allowed negative thoughts to fill my head. I started saying to myself "this will not be read". Yes, that negative voice was talking to me and it almost changed my God given destiny. The whisper kept calling and talking to me. I was bothered that I started another project that I have yet to complete. Thankfully, I had written the statement below to remind me that the DIVINE had answered my prayer and has planted his plan in my mind. This is why I advise you to write any and everything down because when you need encouragement the most it just might be found.

My written words 1/30/2018

As a DISRUPTER I want to become known for my passion to help people know better to do better, it all happens in the MIND. When my spirit is no longer earthbound and has gone on to glory, I want it to be said that I was responsible for millions of people changing their mindset and are living better lives because of the God in me. All I did was simply deliver his message. So, I'm on a journey to help all people but especially, my people, black people, I will become a dominant voice, a messenger that my people will recognize when it comes to elevated thinking -**HIGHER THOUGHT PRINCIPLES** which can literally change lives! MF 01.30.18, 6:03AM

Affirmations
Speak it and Live it!

Affirmation – as defined by Dictionary.com

Something that is affirmed;

a statement or proposition that is declared to be true.

5 Affirmations to Recite Daily
to Get Your MIND RIGHT" So That YOU Can LIVE RIGHT!

When you THINK and LIVE RIGHT
YOU can confidently do YOU and pursue YOUR dreams.

Affirm Daily
"I am an awesome child of GOD"

"I am loving, and kind. I have the Mind of Christ"

"There are many gifts and talents within me the world has yet to see"

"It is in me to accomplish GREAT things"

"I so value what I do. I am blessed to be a blessing. I'm so grateful for blessings bestowed up me"

Recommended Bible Verses
I Focus on these to help me to keep MY MIND RIGHT!

"BUT We have the Mind of Christ"

1st Corinthians 2:16

"A man's gifts makes room for him and brings him before great men"

Proverbs 18:16

"Whoever heeds instruction is on the path to life…"

Proverbs 10:17

"Where there is no guidance, a people falls, but in an abundance of counselors there is safety."

Proverbs 11:14

"Commit your way to the LORD; trust in him, and he will act."

Psalm 37:5

"A wise son hears his father's instruction…"

Proverbs 13:1

"Whoever despises the word brings destruction to himself, but he who reveres the commandment will be rewarded."

Proverbs 13:13

"Poverty and disgrace come to him who ignores instruction, but whoever heeds reproof is honored."

Proverbs 13:18

THE HOLY BIBLE

The Ultimate Book of Instruction

"We all take from it because it is the BOOK OF ALL BOOKS"

I am Michelle and as you read, you see

I take from it too!

Positive Mindset Resources

Websites that Positively Affect your Mind!

FaithFocusFlow.com

InTouch.org – Dr. Charles Stanley

Munroeglobal.com – Dr. Myles Munroe

JoelOsteen.com

DavidJeremiah.org

ThePottersHouse.org

Hillsong.com

BibleGateWay.com

Apps that Positively Affect your Mind!

Motivation Daily & Positivity

Hay House Daily Affirmations

ThinkUp

Thank you to the DIVINE

for placing this revelation in my MIND!

MINDSET

MINDSET

MINDSET

Thank you, LORD, for entrusting me with a specific word to change MENTALITIES. You have so blessed me with many gifts and talents.

I am your Michelle, and I am eternally grateful!

About Me
I am Michelle
Guided by the DIVINE
"Our Lord and Savior Jesus Christ"

~

Daughter of Lois, Mother of Toami, Sister Friend to Many, Aunty to Host of Nieces and Nephews

More about me ~

- *Mentor, Mind Coach , Image Consultant,*
- *Founder of The Mentality Institute and Grow With a Coach Now.com /*
  www.growwithacoachnow.com
- *Published Author of 2 books*
- *Licensed Cosmetologist*
- *Former Corporate Systems Trainer, Business Analyst, and IT Professional*

~ Survivor of Many Things ~

Let's Connect

I would love to inspire and support you

on your mindset reset journey.

email michellewhitby@yahoo.com

www.michellewhitby.com

I cannot wait to meet YOU!

and

Host a Live (PDG)
Personal Development Gathering

~A.K.A~

"Workshop"

I know you will be a Success Hostess and if you say
YES to hosting a gathering you will

receive the following:

FREE
30 Days of Private Mental Mentorship / Coaching Sessions

FREE
RE-Fashioning "Beauty RE-DO"
This a total makeover of YOU from head to toe to match
your NEW MINDSET. You are doing the work to AD'Dress
your inside, now you need to "Refresh" your outside. As a
Licenses Image Consultant, I will share my expertise and
lead you in the direction of your future success.
When it comes to dress….
"The Mind and Body Must Mesh for Optimal Success" ™

FREE
5 Books to share with your loved ones. We will sow seeds of
each one reach one, teach one!

Thank YOU!

And…

As you continue your life's journey my prayer for you is a
multitude of continued blessings flow your way.

Peace and Blessings, Michelle

www.ingramcontent.com/pod-product-compliance
Lightning Source LLC
Chambersburg PA
CBHW051348150726
48000CB00003B/1093